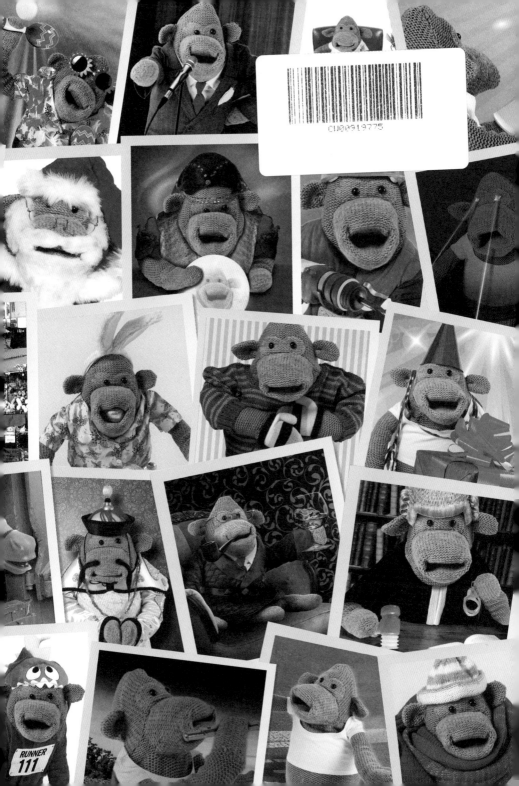

RUNNER
111

MONKEY

A Monkey Walked into a Bar

Published in 2014
by Igloo Books Ltd
Cottage Farm
Sywell
NN6 0BJ
www.igloobooks.com

Monkey TM & © Comic Relief Ltd. 2014

Additional images supplied courtesy of Thinkstock, Getty Images.

HUN001 0814
2 4 6 8 10 9 7 5 3 1
ISBN 978-1-78343-615-6

Printed and manufactured in China

MONKEY

A Monkey Walked into a Bar

igloobooks

My comedy inspiration...
ME!

−Contents−

-Funnyword -

"Monkey walked into a bar, sat down and was bought a banana milkshake by the blond across the bar. Monkey accepted the drink and said, 'Thanks, Boris.' "

Barman

No one likes a laugh more than I do. I suppose I'm lucky to have what are traditionally called 'funny bones' (although I don't actually have what are traditionally called 'bones').

In fact, you'd be surprised at how many times I walk into a room and people burst out laughing. Without me even having to open my mouth! I guess I'm just naturally funny.

As I once told Bruce Forsyth, "You've either got it or you haven't, but there's no harm in trying even if you haven't". And, fair play to Brucie, he took my advice and he's still hanging on in there.

In this book, I'm going to try and teach you, the reader, how to be funny. Chances are that you're not funny at all. You want to be, but you're not.

You try to tell jokes that you've heard other, funnier people tell effortlessly and you end up getting the words in the wrong order, or dribbling out of the corner of your mouth, or holding on to a nearby table in order to stop yourself from collapsing in embarrassment.

This book is for you. It is packed with jokes that you'll be able to entertain crowds of people with, and I'll even teach you how to tell them, so that people won't throw large, heavy objects at you when all you want to do is make them laugh.

Trust me on that one, I learned that one the hard way.

Monkey
x

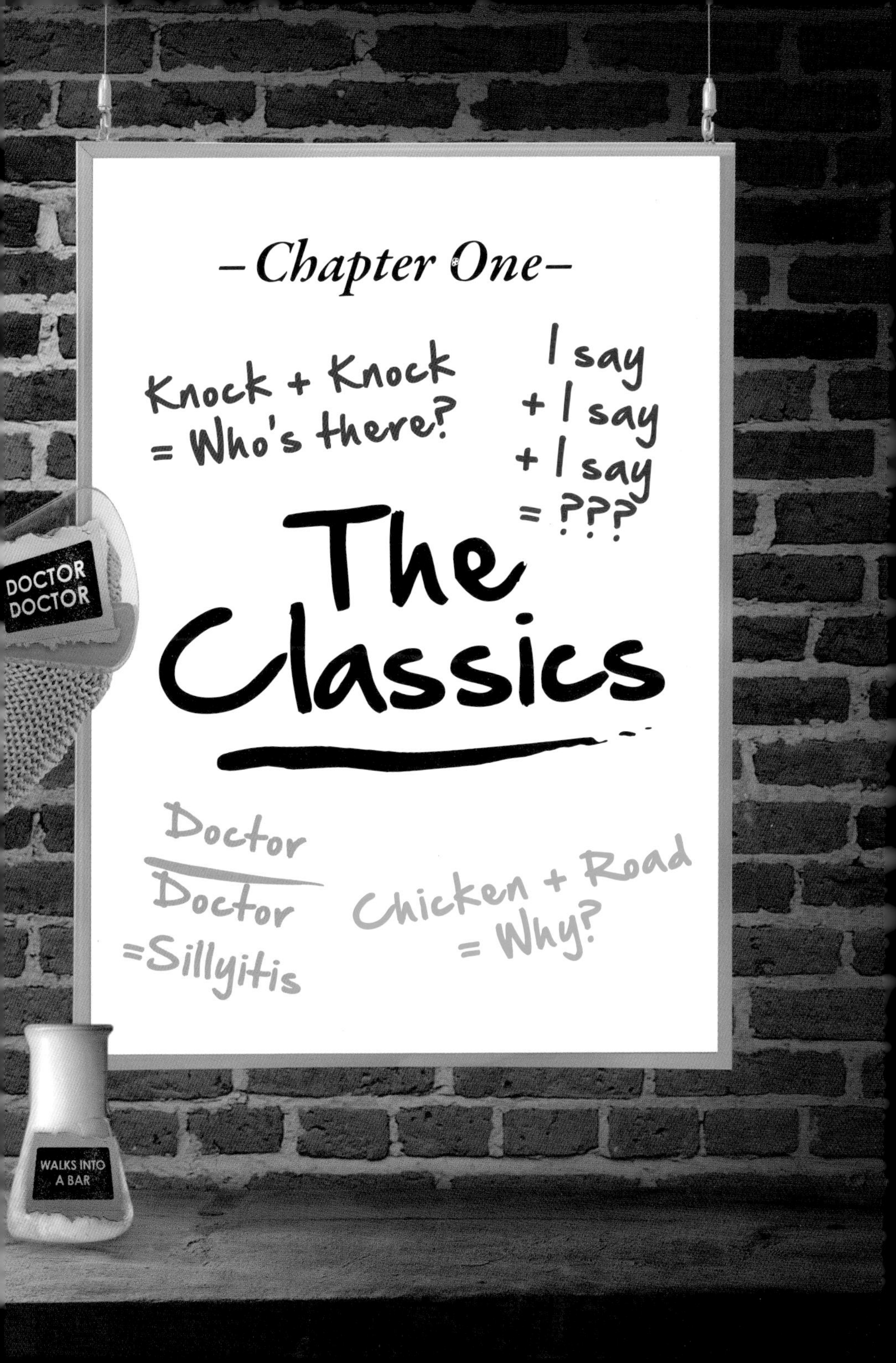

– Chapter One–

Knock + Knock
= Who's there?

I say
+ I say
+ I say
= ???

The Classics

Doctor
Doctor
= Sillyitis

Chicken + Road
= Why?

DOCTOR DOCTOR

WALKS INTO A BAR

Everyone knows that comedy is subjective and that it is hard to write a joke that is a 'classic' and loved by everyone. In 2010, this was voted as one of the funniest jokes of all time…

A woman gets on a bus with her baby. The bus driver says, "Ugh, that's the ugliest baby I've ever seen!" The woman walks to the rear of the bus and sits down, fuming. She says to a man next to her, "The bus driver just insulted me!" The man replies, "What! You go up there and give him what for. Go on, I'll hold your monkey for you."

I don't find that funny. I don't find that funny at all.

Let us explore the classic genre of jokes that involves the name of a monkey who has got an object on his head. These timeless classics work on so many levels. Monkeys are almost always funny and objects on heads are rarely not hilarious.

What do you call a monkey with a spade on his head?
Doug

What do you call a monkey without a spade on his head?
Douglas

What do you call a monkey with a seagull on his head?
Cliff

What do you call a monkey with a car on his head?
Jack

What do you call a monkey with a lavatory on his head?
Lou

What do you call a monkey with a plank of wood on his head?
Edward

What do you call a monkey with two planks of wood on his head?
Edward Wood

What do you call a monkey with three planks of wood on his head?
Edward Woodward

What do you call a monkey with four planks of wood on his head?
I don't know, but Edward Woodward would

There are even some deviations where the monkey *doesn't* have an object on his head. The writers of these jokes must have known they were taking a huge risk, but I think it paid off for them.

What do you call a monkey in a brown paper suit?
Russell

What do you call a monkey with no arms and no legs in a swimming pool?
Bob

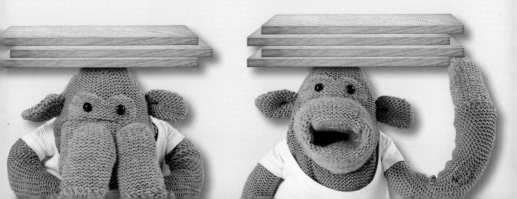

I could go on, but I won't. Mainly because the other ones I've got written down are awful. Let us turn our attention instead to the 'doctor, doctor' genre of jokes.

It's a little-known fact that 'doctor, doctor' jokes originally starred my good self, which is how they came to be so popular. Obviously. But somewhere, somehow, they were hijacked. Yes, *hijacked* by a group of jealous doctors, who started a vindictive whispering campaign and somehow persuaded people that the jokes should be about medical professionals. The cheek!

My account of events is 100% true and you should not question me because I have very powerful lawyers, and I might also have the power of hypnosis. That's for me to know and you to worry about. You *did* buy this book specifically to be threatened by its author in the opening chapter, didn't you?

Good.

Anyway, I digress. Here, presented in their original form, are some of the greatest 'Monkey, Monkey' jokes of all time. I'm sure you'll agree that they're far better starring me than some stupid, glory-seeking doctors.

Monkey, Monkey, I feel like a pair of curtains.
For goodness sake, pull yourself together.

Monkey, Monkey, I feel terrible!
What are the symptoms?
They're a yellow, animated family.

Monkey, Monkey, I think I'm shrinking!
Now, settle down. You'll just have to be a little patient.

Monkey, Monkey, I keep seeing images of Mickey Mouse and Donald Duck!
I see, and how long have you been having these Disney spells?

Monkey, Monkey, I snore so loudly I keep myself awake.
Have you tried sleeping in another room?

Monkey, Monkey, I feel like a sheep.
Oh dear, that sounds baaaaaaaaaa-d!

Strangely, about the same time that my 'Monkey, Monkey' jokes were hijacked by the bitter, spiteful, needy doctors, a spate of 'Monkey-in-law' jokes started being traded on the underground gag market. They had been changed from their original 'mother-in-law' format. I'm pretty sure that those twisted, jealous medics were behind it.

We're living in modern, forward-thinking times now and 'mother-in-law' jokes just aren't funny any more. Here are a few corrupted, underground, black-market gags.

What's the best way to talk to your Monkey-in-law?
Through a medium.

They say every woman has her price. I've got a Monkey-in-law you can have cheap.

My Monkey-in-law is so ugly that a peeping Tom knocked on her door and asked her to close the curtains.

See?
Not funny.
Hurtful.
Mean.

What is the appeal behind these classic jokes? What makes us go back to them time and time again? I decided that I should do some *science* in order to work out what it's all about (and the publisher said I'd look good in a white scientist's coat, too).

I got in touch with the government's Ministry of Comedy and did some valuable research with them in an attempt to see if these jokes worked in real life. We gathered together an audience of specially selected laughter fans and ushered them into a darkened theatre.

I walked on stage into the spotlight and carefully placed a spade on to my head.

"My name is Doug," I said.

They all laughed. I then removed the spade.

"My name is Douglas."

Again there was tittering in the auditorium.

I then produced a seagull from a cage and placed it on my head, telling the crowd that my name was now Cliff. Once more, they giggled.

This was scientific proof that these jokes are funny because they are based in truth. I had cracked the secret of comedy.

Tickets for my 74-date, national 'Things On My Head' tour are now available at all the usual outlets, and there will be a DVD and Blu-ray released in time for next Christmas.

WHERE FUNNY BEGAN...

JUST WHO WAS THE VERY FIRST COMEDIAN? CHARLIE CHAPLIN? TOMMY COOPER? OF COURSE NOT. COMEDY IS ALMOST AS OLD AS MANKIND ITSELF. IN FACT, BOFFINS RECKON THAT COMEDY EXISTED WAY BACK IN THE STONE AGE.

THOSE VERY BOFFINS RECENTLY DISCOVERED SOME CAVE PAINTINGS, WHICH SHOW A HAIRY CAVEMAN STANDING IN FRONT OF A CROWD OF ONLOOKERS. IN IT, HE IS RESTING ON A LONG STICK, WHICH SEEMS TO RESEMBLE A MICROPHONE STAND, AND HE IS HOLDING A BONE UP TO HIS MOUTH. WE CAN ONLY ASSUME THAT THIS IS SOME KIND OF EARLY VERSION OF A MICROPHONE.

IF WE ARE IN ANY DOUBT AS TO WHETHER THIS IS A DRAWING OF ONE OF THE VERY FIRST STAND-UP COMEDY PERFORMANCES, WE NEED ONLY LOOK AT THE INSCRIPTION SCRAWLED ABOVE THE CRUDE, KIDDY-STYLE ART.

"TAKE MY MOTHER-IN-LAW, NO, PLEASE, SOMEONE TAKE HER."

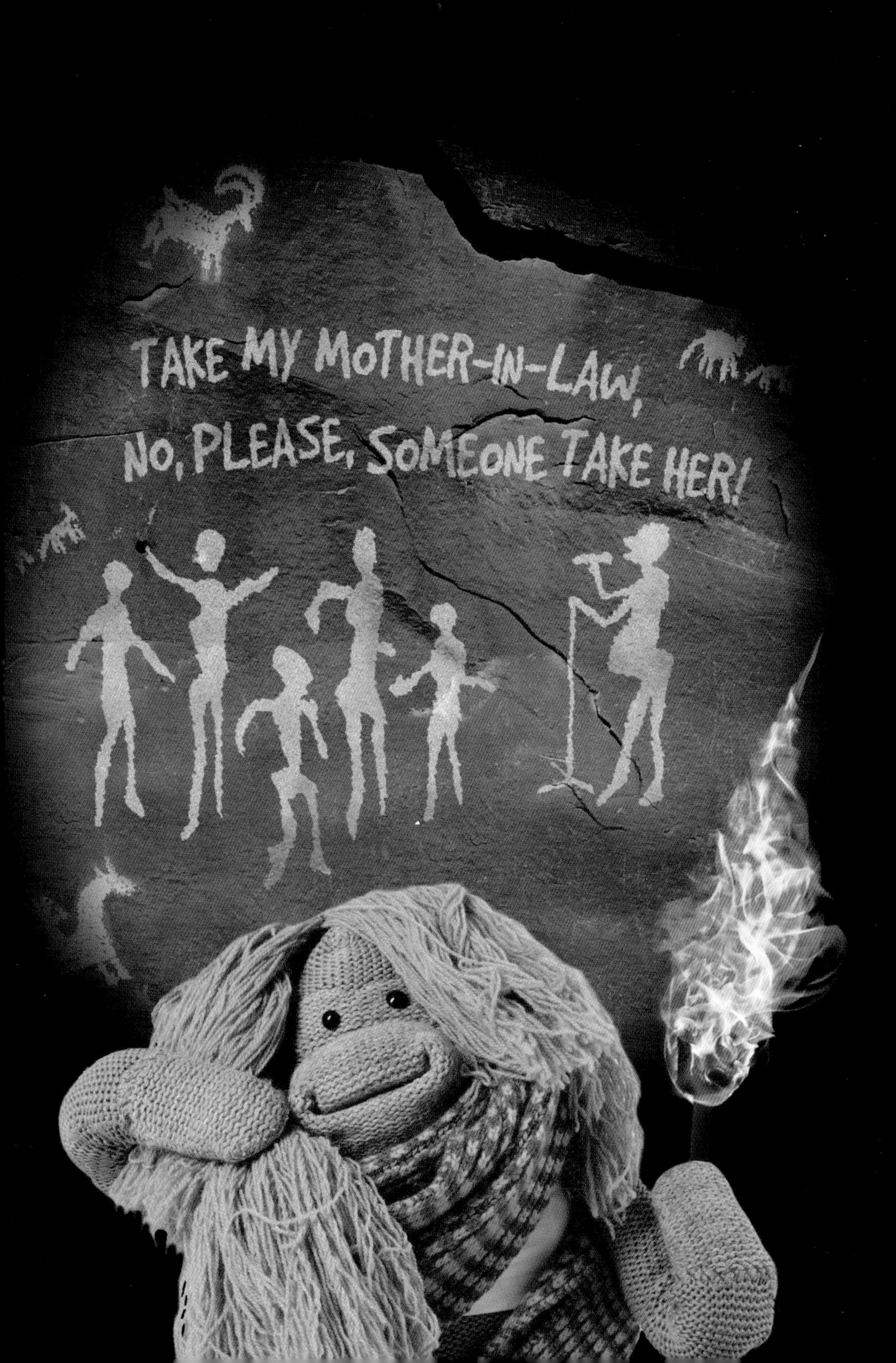
TAKE MY MOTHER-IN-LAW,
NO, PLEASE, SOMEONE TAKE HER!

– *Chapter Two* –

the art of the one-liner

Who uttered the immortal phrase, "If you can make 'em laugh you can make 'em wallpaper your spare room for you"? It was me, just then, right off the top of my head. That's how witty I am. Deal with it.

It's the kind of devastating one-liner that I can come up with at the drop of a hat, and one of the reasons why I've been voted the world's funniest woollen character by the Stuffed Comedy Council for the past nine years.

The one-liner is the most devastating weapon in the arsenal of the funny funster. Used correctly, it can reduce an audience to quivering wrecks of hilarity-wobbling jelly-people, rendered helpless by the jaw-dropping gag that has just been delivered right into their faces.

Or, if you find yourself under pressure, you can use a one-liner to diffuse a tricky situation, becoming the instant king of the witty comebacks and seeing off all bullies, oppressors and anyone who just doesn't agree with you.

If you're smart enough, you can take a tried-and-trusted one-liner and pass it off as your own. Just make sure you get the words in the right order and don't start to sweat profusely as you do it.

Back when I was taking baby steps in the world of showbiz megastardom, I was lucky enough to land the role of Choco, the cheeky clown-monkey with a well-known ventriloquist. I say 'lucky' but it turned out to be a nightmare.

And when I say that the ventriloquist was 'well-known', I mean that he was well-known to the fruit-market police, owing to his long list of fruit-snatching misdemeanours. Most of our performances took place in the communal areas of old folks' homes, near popular supermarkets. Why old folks' homes? you ask. We could have filled a moderately sized village hall, but not all village halls have kitchens with smoothie makers. Old folks' homes on the other hand, with their need for nutritious, puréed food, had smoothie makers in abundance!

Evening shows were a waste of time – his excessive intake of sugar-rich smoothies made him hyper, like a small child after a gallon of fizzy pop. Audiences would become enraged at his shoddy displays and at times he would leave me to fend for myself, as he ran round and round in circles. In the end, the roles were reversed, with me doing the voice of the ventriloquist *and* myself, as he sprinted past every few seconds.

Without doubt, the worst bit about it all was the hecklers. "You stink! Not your act – your breath!" shouted one audience member at my handler. She had a point; he did stink. Over time, his smoothie addiction had rotted his teeth, which made opening his mouth not just eye-opening, but somewhat pungent to the front row. There was only one thing for it. I had to go nuclear on her, pull out my best wit-weapon and destroy her in front of the crowd (who were by this point roaring with mocking laughter).

I channelled my inner Winston Churchill and, throwing my voice into the mouth of the sprinting ventriloquist, I shouted, "Madam, I may be energetic, smelly and lacking a perfect smile, but in the morning I will probably still be running and have morning fruit breath. You, on the other hand, will still be…" I paused, for effect, although it was also mainly to decide what to say next. "You will still be… a charming and delightful young lady." She had no comeback to that – I had silenced her with kindness.

Speaking of silence, the ventriloquist and myself came to a premature parting a few weeks later when he ran off to open his own smoothie shop in Melon Bridge, Devon.

I thought things would be easier in my next job as a department store Santa Claus over the festive season. Everyone loves Santa, right? Wrong. As I was soon to find out the hard way.

There I was on my first day in the throne, sat on a festively wrapped box so that the kids could actually see me (yes, I know I'm not the traditional Santa Claus sort of shape). In came the first kid, dragging his shoes along the ground and picking his nose. I sensed danger.

He strode over and looked down at me. I estimated his age was something between 15 and 19. "Is that a real beard, old man?" he roared while slurping on an ice-cream cone (I know, in winter! I had a bad feeling about this child). He then forcefully tugged at my artificial face-fur. I recoiled in horror, amazed at the complete lack of respect from this dewy-eyed tyke. It was obvious that a snappy one-liner was required here.

"Please stop touching me! I have a medical condition that makes me wet myself if my beard gets pulled!" I yelped in his face. Okay, so it wasn't a line worthy of one of the greatest wits or raconteurs of our time, but it got the job done.

The youth stood back, looked me up and down, and dropped a little bit of ice-cream out of his cone, which went all over my lovely, clean beard. Once my suspension period had elapsed, I continued in my role as Santa for the remainder of the Yuletide season. Victory was mine.

Pretty much.

It was all a learning curve for me though, and by the time I cracked it big-style in Hollywood, I was untouchable, my ready-wit on show for all to see. My shining moment came on the red carpet at the premiere of my hit movie, *Spy Shark Prison Escape 7*, a few years ago when I was pranked by a comedy, fake reporter.

You haven't seen *Spy Shark Prison Escape 7*? Friend, you have truly missed out. It's a cult classic. In it, I played Dusty Fresh, a hip-hop wordsmith who had been imprisoned after rapping rude words in his sleep. Viewers were kept guessing whether I was a spy or a shark right up until the end of the movie. Critics called it, "A seminal aqua-based espionage, genre-bending classic" and they also said kind things about it too!

Anyway, as I walked down the red carpet, a 'reporter' stuck his microphone in my face and said, "Monkey, have you got a message for your fans?" to which I replied "Yes, I love each and every one of you!" So far, so good.

Then, he stared at his question card and said, "I'm sorry I read that wrong. It says, do you have a message for your *fan*? Singular. As in just one." My face fell. I knew I was on the brink of being made a fool, but I remained cool and hit back with the ultimate zinger.

"Your mum's my fan," I deadpanned. He was destroyed and I was the star of the night. You've either got it, or you haven't.

So that's the one-liner then. Taking you from zero to power-LOL in just a few seconds – the turbo-powered, sports-car of comedy.

What's the difference between outlaws and in-laws?

OUTLAWS ARE

WANTED!

Love is Blind!
Only marriage
opens your eyes

*You can pick
your friends, you
can pick your
nose, but you
can't pick your
friend's nose!*

CHI MP

-Chapter Three-

WORD PLAY

If each day
is a gift -
where can
I return
Mondays?

DAVID
BOWIE

Our English language is a curious and sprawling beast – as I just demonstrated by calling it a curious and sprawling beast. We've got thousands of different words with so many permutations that it's easy to form a sentence and be pretty sure that it's never been uttered by anyone in the history of everything. Such as…

The original spotty frog flew its photocopied miracle train past the dog dentist and into David Bowie's mink Christmas pigeonhole, where plastic berries and rotten fur were growing.

See? Not that hard is it? Try and come up with your own original sentence and maybe write it in a birthday card to someone you love. It'll confuse them on their special day, but they'll never forget it.

43

The English language is also filled with strange, weird and downright funny sayings. But where did they all come from? It's said that William Shakespeare was the father of modern English and he is believed to have contributed about 3,000 words and phrases to the language. Here are my favourites, but how based in reality are they?

"Knock, knock! Who's there?"

Boom! Not only has the Bard introduced a new phrase, he's even invented a classic genre of joke that has survived for hundreds of years. In fact, it was my two-year-old niece's first ever kind of joke. It went:

Knock, knock!

Who's there?

Orange.

Orange who?

Orange silver.

Okay, so it needs a bit of work, but it's pretty good for a first attempt.

A wild goose chase We use this one almost every day, but do we ever stop to think what it means? Are we chasing a wild goose? Is it chasing *us*? Just how wild is it and what will it do if it catches us? I don't think I'm going to be able to use this phrase any more and I'm terrified that I'll be dreaming about wild geese tonight. Thanks a bunch, Shakespeare.

Wear your heart on your sleeve This is another one that we use regularly, but what if we took it literally? What if we were able to prove to someone that we were showing our true feelings by ripping out our hearts and wearing them on our sleeves? Would the heart continue to beat? Wouldn't that be off-putting? How would we get the blood stains out of our shirts? Thanks again, Shakespeare.

Vanish into thin air Another one that doesn't really stack up when put under intense Monkey scrutiny. Where does one find the thinnest air? High above sea level, of course. By that reckoning, if someone vanishes into thin air, simply climb the nearest tall mountain and you'll find them straight away. Poor show, Shakespeare.

The world's mine oyster Just one oyster? That's a bit miserly is it not, Will? Compare the size of the world to the size of an oyster. They're two completely different things. Also, eating oysters has always seemed a bit like eating bogeys, to me. No thanks, Mr. Shakespeare.

Not slept one wink Another piece of gobbledegook from the supposed king of the English language. I've heard of sleepwalking and sleeptalking, and I even had a friend who would go down to his garage and play darts while he was still asleep, but sleepwinking? That's just weird. Major Shakespeare fail.

Puking Urrgh. That's *quite* enough thank you, Mr. Shakespeare.

VANISH
into
THIN
AIR

MONKEY
POWER
WASHING
POWDER

VANISH
into
THIN
AIR

So then, how did Shakespeare manage to contribute so much to the English language? Swollen-brained scholars all seem to agree that he was simply the most intelligent, imaginative and creative person alive in those days. Me, I'm pretty sure that he's someone from the future who built a time machine and travelled back to 1589, whereupon he started writing plays filled with phrases that we all use nowadays.

I don't know how, but I suspect he managed to make himself a load of money out of it as well. If I'm lying, he can come back to the present day and I'll see him in court. *Are you reading this Mr. Future Shakespeare? Do you accept my challenge?*

Now we wait for his response. While we do, I've been thinking about what the modern-day equivalent of Shakespearean language is. Who are the people that are coming up with brand new words and phrases and releasing them into the English language as though they're some kind of poisonous gas?

It's the businessmen and businesswomen (and they're *definitely* in it for the money). They're the motley crew responsible for this sorry lot:

Think outside the box   Which box? Why do we need to get into a box in order to think? Why can't we just sit down in a comfy chair with a cup of tea and some soothing music playing? What if the thinker is scared of confined spaces? Business idiots!

Blue-sky thinking   This is supposed to be ideas that are not connected to the current reality. Here's some blue-sky thinking; take all of your blue-sky ideas, write them down on some blue-sky paper, tape them to a rocket and fire them into the blue sky. Ahhh, that's better. Stupid business idiots.

Bleeding edge   Because cutting edge doesn't cut it any more, we now have to have bleeding edge instead. I'm going to wear my heart on my sleeve here and ask who's going to be responsible for cleaning up all the blood afterwards.

Burning platform   When a business goes wrong, it is said to be on a burning platform, like an oil platform. If any of these office-dwelling business idiots were ever really on a burning platform, they'd wet themselves and cry for their mummies.

Drill down   More oil-drilling jargon, supposedly about exploring an idea further and getting more information about it. Working in a job where you get to use a big drill is much better than being a big-time businessperson. They're just showing their jealousy here.

Learnings   As in 'things we've learned', or maybe 'data', or 'evidence'. Don't say 'learnings' – you sound ridiculous.

Low-hanging fruit   No one knows what this really means. They just say it when there's a quiet moment in a meeting. Stupid, stupid business idiots.

I could write an entire book about the origin of words and what they all mean, but I'm pretty sure that this chapter has been a bit of an ordeal for you, so I won't.

Time for me to vanish into thin air!

What's the best way to carve wood?

WHITTLE BY WHITTLE

–Chapter Four–

The Best Monkey Speech

Dig, if you will, a picture, of me done up in my best tuxedo, tapping the side of a glass with a spoon and coughing. I'm sitting in the middle of a long table in a large room, drinks have been flowing and good times are being had by all.

Now it is my time to shine. Now it is time for I, Monkey, to take centre stage and captivate the room with my dazzling wit and sparkling repartee. Yes, I'm at another one of my enjoyable after-dinner speaking appearances. And lucrative – oh, they're lucrative, too.

Everyone puts down their champagne, or milkshake and hangs on to my every word for the next 45 minutes. Although in truth, I only speak for about 18 minutes. The rest of the time is filled up with gales of laughter from the assembled throng, repeated rounds of applause and the attendance of paramedics as one, or two people pass out from their Monkey-induced hysterics. Standard Thursday evening, really.

But how come it's little old *me* who is fully booked up to do after-dinner speeches between now and June 2023, and not *you*? There are lots of reasons and I'm going to enlighten you, so that, maybe, you can one day be as good at public speaking as I am. Maybe.

Unfortunately, there's a whole host of reasons why you might be asked to stand up in front of a crowded room and be mildly amusing. Chances are that it will happen to you at one point, or another.

BEST MAN'S SPEECH

Congratulations! If you've been asked to do this, it means that you've got a chum who deems you special enough to speak at his wedding. That, or you're really good at telling jokes and he wants to bask in your reflected glory.

Either way, you could be on to a winner. Get it right and all the men at the wedding will want to buy you drinks, while the women will want to kiss you on the lip part of your face. But, get it wrong and you'll probably need either a lawyer, or a trip to the local accident and emergency department. So, do your research (on the groom's childhood *and* the location of the nearest hospital).

SPEECH AT YOUR OLD SCHOOL

Chances are that you'll only be asked to do this if you've made something of yourself. If you spend your days swearing at complete strangers in internet chatrooms, or have just completed a community service order for a mild fraud, your old headmaster won't be on the blower.

But if you do get invited back for the old school talk, focus on things that have made you the success that you are today. Don't mention the time you abseiled off the school roof using five kites that you'd glued together. Yes, it shows initiative, but it might give the kids the wrong idea.

AWARDS ACCEPTANCE SPEECH

Bit of a niche one this, and it probably only applies to myself and some of my dearest celebrity pals. (Hi, Tom, Meryl, Tom, Tom, Dame Judi, Tom and Tom, I know you'll all be reading this, possibly all together in the VIP room at the Hollywood Showbiz Lounge).

The trick here is to keep it short and succinct. Only thank people who are blood relatives, or who you've seen naked. No one else in your life is worthy of your thanks. Also, be humble. Don't grab the award from the host and punch the air with it, shouting, "In your face [*insert name of your oldest and deadliest nemesis*]! That's for all the times you [*insert dreadful deeds carried out against you by said nemesis*]!" No one likes a show off.

COURT APPEARANCE

This is a more sombre example of public speaking and the opportunities for you to generate a few belly laughs will be tricky, and few and far between. If you're a witness, keep cool and calm, and answer all the questions to the fullest of your knowledge. If you're the defendant, don't use foul language and don't pick your nose. If you're the judge, make sure your wig isn't on back to front.

So, given that you might have to appear at one of those events at some time in your life, here are my Five Golden Rules of Public Speaking:

1. BE CONFIDENT If you're planning to take an audience and hold it in the palm of your hand, there's no room for nerves. You could use that tried-and-trusted method of imagining your audience naked, but if it's a room full of old-aged pensioners, that might put you off a bit. As for myself, I always imagine the audience as an army of oversized ants dressed in nappies and curly rainbow-coloured wigs. If they're a *really* tricky crowd, I imagine myself destroying them all with laser beams that shoot out of my eyes. Is that weird? It probably is, isn't it?

2. KNOW YOUR AUDIENCE If you're speaking to a room full of vegans, don't litter your routine with tales of when you used to work in a butcher's shop as a teenager. If you're addressing a Steve Davis

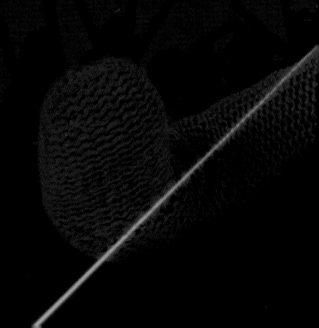

fan convention, don't talk about your admiration for Stephen Hendry. If you're talking to a group of nine-year-old Cub Scouts, don't tell them the joke about the nuns, the bar of soap and the swings. Actually, don't ever tell anyone that joke – it's disturbing.

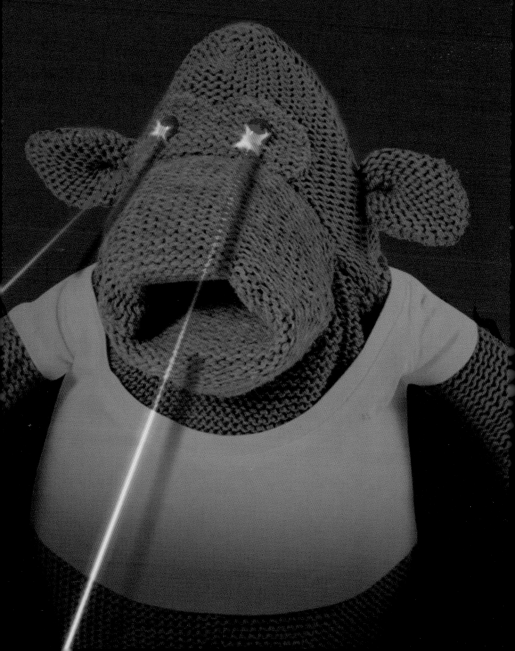

3. DON'T MAKE IT UP AS YOU GO ALONG

Obviously, this rule doesn't apply to myself as I'm a battle-hardened veteran, with thousands of successful speeches under my imaginary belt. At the very least, put together a list of topics that you want to talk about, in bullet point form. Just as importantly, don't get the piece of paper mixed up with your shopping list, or car tax renewal form – you could be in for a tough gig if you do.

4. KEEP IT SIMPLE   Your job is to say words and entertain the audience. Do not attempt to rap parts of your speech. Do not attempt to do mild conjuring. Do not use helium for squeaky voice comedy effects. Do not take the opportunity to settle scores if you spot your oldest and deadliest nemesis in the crowd.

Common sense
Extra sense
Monkey scents

Shrugs? Cardigans?
Capes?
Bearded tits
Bearded lizards
Bearded monkeys?

Margarine M
Ghoulash..
Nake
N

Yew trees
Operations
Rubber trees
Rubber bands
Choirs

5. DON'T BE TOO GOOD AT IT Look, I make a very tidy living from this sort of thing. In fact, between myself and Jonathan Ross, we've more or less got the whole scene carved up, and we don't want any young pretenders muscling in on our action. Jonathan is pretty handy with nunchucks and, although I may be small, I'm a black belt in giving Chinese burns. Know your place and you'll be okay.

NOTE: Lawyers, is that okay as a threat?

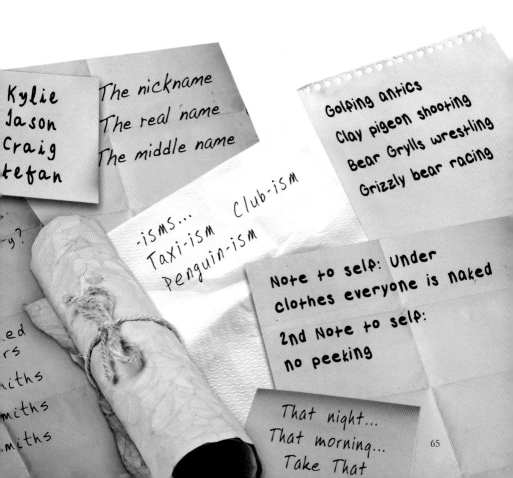

A monkey walked into a bar... OUCH!

Stand-up, Sit-down

The phone rang the other day. I picked it up and a voice on the other end said, "Monkey? Hi, it's Jerry here." I was taken aback. I'd never spoken to the legendary cartoon mouse before, and what's more, his voice sounded lower than when I'd heard it on those few occasions that he'd spoken in his hilarious short films.

"Oh! Hi, Jerry. How's Tom?" I stuttered.

To which he replied, "What? It's Jerry. Jerry Seinfeld."

Ah. So it was arguably the greatest stand-up comedian in the world that was calling me. Sometimes you have to ride the disappointments that life throws at you.

Never mind. I sat and listened as Jerry bent my ear with endless talk about the art of stand-up comedy, for about an hour. He does this now and again. I think he finds it reassuring.

But why did he think it was appropriate to call little old me? Well, probably because I'm one of the most influential names in stand-up comedy today. But you knew that, right?

It all started one night, a couple of decades ago. I was on my way back from the fancy-dress, ping-pong club that I frequented back then. I was dressed as Henry VIII and had narrowly lost a frantic match against Spider-Man. Maybe I'd chosen the wrong costume for ping-pong, what with the large hat and fat suit, but hey, hindsight is a wonderful thing.

I wandered past a comedy club that I'd never seen before and, feeling sorry for myself, ventured inside. It was an 'open mic' night – a chance for talented amateurs and hopeless braggarts to get on stage and chance their arm with some lousy jokes they'd written on the backs of their hands.

After I sat through four terrible, terrible wannabe comedians, I decided that I could do better myself, and clambered up on stage. I'm too small to be seen when standing up on a stage, so a nice lady brought me a stool.

Then, nightmare! My mind went blank as I realised that I didn't know any jokes. Rather than be humiliated and trudge off stage to the sound of embarrassed silence, I told the tale of my fancy-dress, ping-pong encounter instead.

Eureka! The entire 17-strong audience whooped and hollered along as I described how Spider-Man had destroyed me over the ping-pong table and I got a standing ovation as I climbed down from my stool and headed back into the audience.

As luck would have it, among those 17 people that night was Dennis St. Contract, one of the most powerful comedy agents in the land. After some hard-fought negotiation (mostly about whether I would prefer to be paid in cash, or bottles of lemonade), I was signed up to his agency and my whirlwind career as a stand-up comedian had begun.

It turned out that I was a natural. All I had to do was talk about my life and the things I enjoyed doing, and rooms full of people would fall about laughing. I had finally found my calling (along with acting, singing, magic, many sports, feats of strength and tests of mental agility – I'm quite the all-rounder).

Within weeks, I was performing at venues across the land, appearing on TV and radio panel shows. I was even the first comedian to play Wembley Stadium. Well, kind of… I got dragged out of the crowd and up on to the stage to dance with Bono during a U2 concert there. That counts.

It *does*.

The stand-up scene is notorious for its competitive nature, and I've seen some fierce rivalries between some of the top names down the years, with scenes of fury that would make your hair curl. I realise how enticing that sounds, so here are my five favourite feuds from my stand-up career. (Some of this may be removed by my lawyers).

1. The time when ███████████ attacked and pinned down ███████████ backstage at The Happy Factory Club in Harrogate, before forcing a whistle up his nose just minutes before he was due to headline on stage. This was following a row over a stolen joke about snakes and ladders. Ever the trooper, ███████████ went on stage regardless, musically whistling out most of his material. Later, the whistle had to be surgically removed.

2. The time when ███████████ tried to make ███████████ ███████ seriously ill by giving him some poisonous berries mixed with fruit juice. This followed a heated debate over how to properly deliver the punchline from a Woody Allen routine from 1965.

3. The time when ███████████ put a microwave oven over the head of ███████████ in the kitchen of Wally's Jolly House in Swindon, before plugging it in and switching it on. The argument was over which of them was contracted to appear fourth on the bill at an upcoming charity show for people with webbed feet. ███████████ was taken to hospital, but later lost most of his hair.

4. The time when ███████████ and ███████████ kidnapped ███████████ and drove him 400 miles in the back of a van to the Shetland Islands and released him stark naked in the middle of a forest in one of the coldest Januarys on record. This followed a

difference of opinion over whether Jasper Carrott was better than Billy Connolly.

5. The time when ███████████████ had a funny turn in the car park of the ███████████ Club in ████████████ and poured ████████████ all over the ███████████████ that belonged to ████████████ (yes, him again) before ███████████████ it as ████████████ looked on, sobbing like a child. That incident was after a row over the ownership of a cheese pasty.

Great times, they really were.

It might seem strange, but one of my favourite things about doing stand-up (while sitting down, obviously) is the banter that you get to share with the audience, in particular, hecklers. Some of my fellow comedians see hecklers as an irritation, but if you handle them properly, you can turn a potentially nasty situation around and make yourself look like even more of a comedy genius than you already are.

For example, if a heckler shouts, "You're about as funny as my nan's haemorrhoids," the perfect comeback is "I'm going to find out where you work, come in on Monday and break wind on your computer, or the tools of your trade."

There, situation diffused and massive laughs had by everyone.

Alternatively, if a heckler shouts, "When's the comedian coming on then, mate?" Simply come back at them with, "I'm going to find out where you live and sign up for a lot of brochures and other marketing literature that you neither want, nor need, to be sent to your address." That usually shuts them up.

Or, if the heckler shouts, "You're just a woollen idiot and everyone here is laughing at you out of a misplaced sense of sympathy," just feign a collapse. Someone will perform first aid on you and you may have to pretend to be ill as you undergo tests in hospital, but the heckler will be overcome with shame and you'll have the last laugh. It also ties in with the golden rule of stand-up comedy – always leave them wanting more.

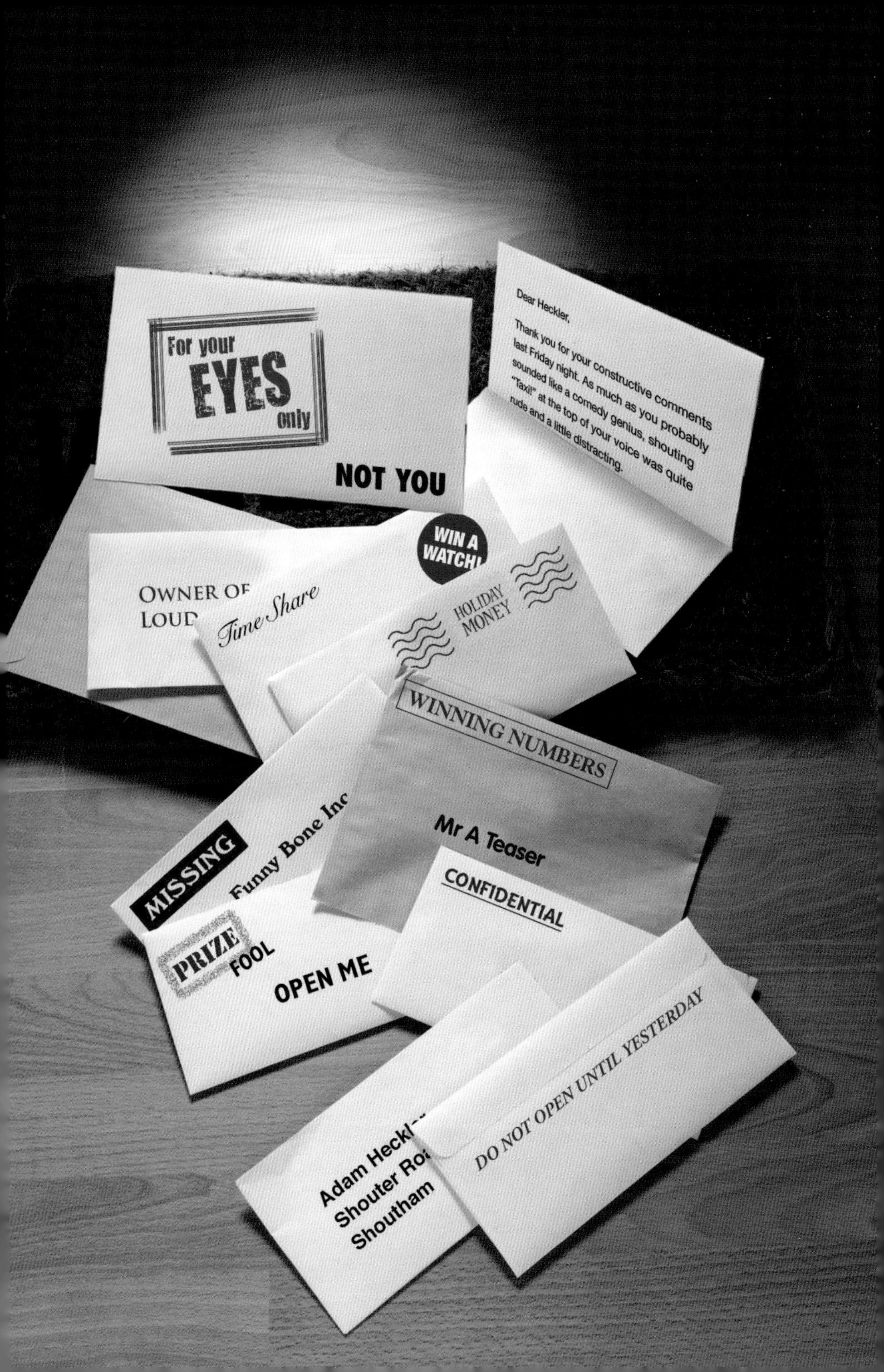

For your
EYES only

NOT YOU

Dear Heckler,

Thank you for your constructive comments last Friday night. As much as you probably sounded like a comedy genius, shouting "Taxi!" at the top of your voice was quite rude and a little distracting.

OWNER OF
LOUD

Time Share

WIN A
WATCH!

HOLIDAY
MONEY

WINNING NUMBERS

MISSING

Funny Bone Inc

Mr A Teaser

PRIZE FOOL

CONFIDENTIAL

OPEN ME

Adam Heckl
Shouter Roa
Shoutham

DO NOT OPEN UNTIL YESTERDAY

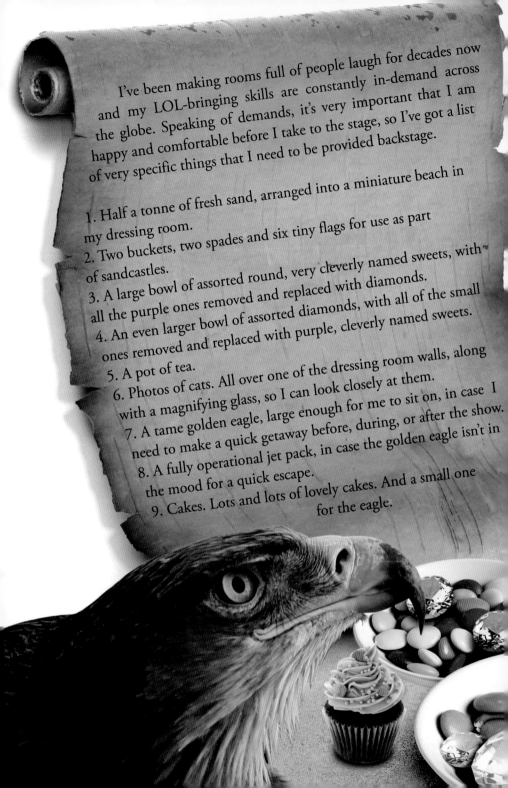

I've been making rooms full of people laugh for decades now and my LOL-bringing skills are constantly in-demand across the globe. Speaking of demands, it's very important that I am happy and comfortable before I take to the stage, so I've got a list of very specific things that I need to be provided backstage.

1. Half a tonne of fresh sand, arranged into a miniature beach in my dressing room.
2. Two buckets, two spades and six tiny flags for use as part of sandcastles.
3. A large bowl of assorted round, very cleverly named sweets, with all the purple ones removed and replaced with diamonds.
4. An even larger bowl of assorted diamonds, with all of the small ones removed and replaced with purple, cleverly named sweets.
5. A pot of tea.
6. Photos of cats. All over one of the dressing room walls, along with a magnifying glass, so I can look closely at them.
7. A tame golden eagle, large enough for me to sit on, in case I need to make a quick getaway before, during, or after the show.
8. A fully operational jet pack, in case the golden eagle isn't in the mood for a quick escape.
9. Cakes. Lots and lots of lovely cakes. And a small one for the eagle.

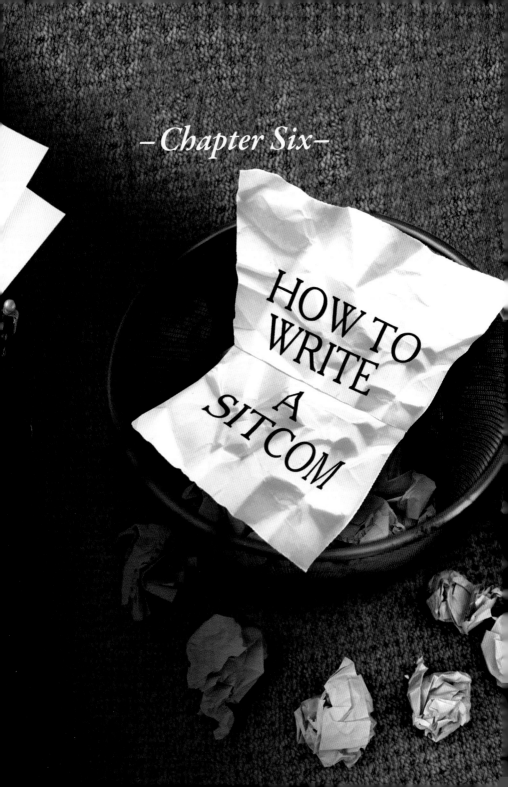

–*Chapter Six*–

HOW TO WRITE A SITCOM

L et us consider the mighty sitcom. Loved by millions of us, it gets its name from the fact that it is the kind of comedy that is best enjoyed while sitting down. Which is perfect for someone like myself, who finds standing up, walking around and generally being active a bit of a chore.

The sitcom is so widely loved because, not only do you get to sit down, you get to laugh as well - if you're lucky. Double bubble, as a friend of mine likes to say sometimes (he's a bit odd).

As a comedy legend, my life has been intertwined with sitcoms and while I am yet to star in a hit one, I've enjoyed hundreds of them over the years. Here, in no particular order, are my top five:

BLACKADDER This is my absolute top favourite of all time. In it, Rowan Atkinson plays a time traveller who appears in different eras and changes the course of history. In my opinion, the fourth and final series was the best. Set in the war, Rowan Blackadder went to Germany and discovered the mystery of Bavarian fashion.

LAST OF THE SUMMER WINE I loved this one as a kid – it was on every Sunday night and I watched it after my bath. Every week, three old men wandered around before building a go-kart out of bits of scrap, which they would then race down a hill. After 43 series, it never got boring!

PORRIDGE Another classic, set in a prison and starring Ronnie Barker of Ronnie & Ronnie fame. This one was so funny that it made me want to go to prison myself. That didn't really work out though – I stole an apple from an orchard and got my head stuck in some railings, and pretty much gave up after that.

THE OFFICE Another classic, although I only found out that it's a sitcom quite recently. I'd always thought it was a proper documentary and that David Brent was a real person, which is quite confusing. Imagine my surprise when I learned the truth about *The Only Way Is Essex*. Did you know that Joey Essex is a real person? It's true. Strange, but true.

BIRDS OF A FEATHER Another big favourite from my younger years. A very funny show, but I have to admit that my hormones were sent a-racing by the delectable sights of Sharon, Tracy and Dorien next door. I had posters of them on my bedroom wall and enjoyed many moments of special teenage feelings while thinking about them.

Making a sitcom isn't a science and for every classic, there are at least three, or four roaring stinkers. Here are the five worst shows that I can remember:

BULL IN A CHINA SHOP In this short-lived flop, a character named Barry Bull inherits a china shop that he doesn't want. His continual neglect, along with a drinking problem, meant that the shop went bust by the end of episode six and no second series was made. Very short on laughs as well.

A STITCH IN TIME In this short-lived flop, a character named Alfred Stitch moves to a sleepy village called Time. Unfortunately, he is a persistent sleepwalker and his nocturnal antics get him into continual trouble. By the end of episode six, Stitch was given £5,000 by the locals to move away and never return. Very short on laughs, no second series was made.

RHYTHM IS A DANCER In this short-lived flop, a character named Karen Rhythm suffers from strange dancing side-effects whenever she takes her hay-fever medication. She appears on a TV talent show and wins, becoming an overnight star. In episode six, she fell overboard while working on a cruise ship and was eaten by a whale. Grotesquely unfunny, no second series was made.

HORSE AND CART In this short-lived flop, Alan Cart inherits a useless racehorse from an uncle. Owing to budget restrictions, we only ever get to see the horse's head in its stable, and it is clearly a puppet. Described by the British Medical Association as 'a trigger for ego-maniacal face-painting', no second series was ever made.

HORSE IN A CHINA SHOP In this short-lived flop, which combined two failed sitcoms, Barry Bull buys a useless horse from Alan Cart, keeping it in his now-ruined china shop. A show that had viewing figures of just 17. A second episode was never made.

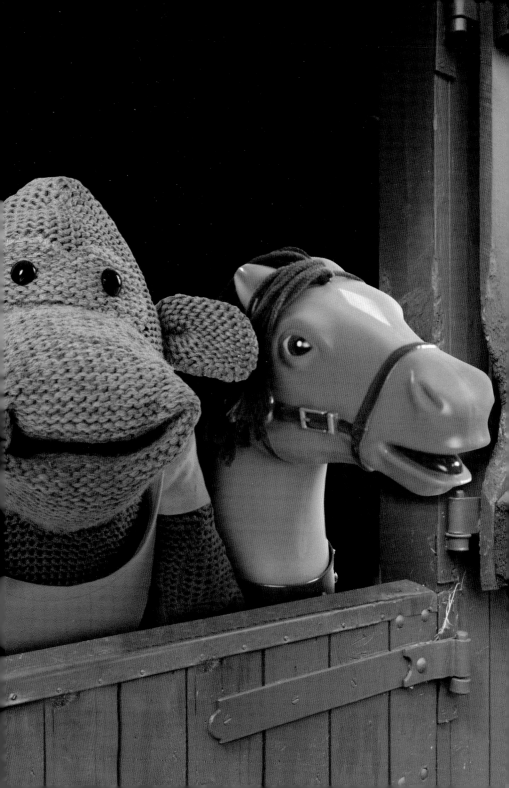

So, how does one go about crafting the perfect sitcom? Coming up with a suitable name for a sitcom is crucial. It needs to entice the viewer, while letting them know what the show is all about. I remember back in 1981, looking forward to the first episode of what I thought was going to be a hilarious sitcom about a gang of really stupid jockeys.

But when I tuned in, it was about some blokes living in a tiny flat in London and trying to make a living through various dodgy means. I don't know how many episodes of *Only Fools and Horses* were eventually made, but it'd have been a lot more if they'd bothered to come up with a proper title.

Next, you need a believable situation, but one that can be ripe with laughter and funny situations. A family filled with different personalities all clashing with each other can be very funny. A family who don't communicate, but throw shoes at each other all the time, is less funny.

Finally, a sitcom is nothing without a great cast. David Jason, myself, Dawn French, Ricky Gervais and Miranda Hart are all great sitcom actors. Get us involved and you can't fail. On the other hand, Simon Cowell, The Incredible Hulk and Ann Widdecombe would probably be less suitable, if you were looking for your dream cast.

I've yet to make the full transition from all-round woollen legend into all-round sitcom legend, but it's not like I haven't tried. I was moments away from landing a role in what was going to be called 'Monkey Behaving Badly' a few years ago, but there was a change of plan at the last minute.

"It's a flatshare sitcom, but you don't actually share the flat with anyone," they said. "We don't think that's going to be particularly entertaining," they said. "We've changed our minds and are going to rework it completely… with men," they said.

I was appalled by this anti-Monkey prejudice and insisted that one of the subsequent *Men Behaving Badly* characters be some kind of simian. I don't know if this had any influence on their creation of the character of Tony.

I never watched it.

It hurt too much.

So, here, with elements taken from my all-time favourites, is my ultimate sitcom of all time, starring *me* of course. Telly bosses, start preparing your blank cheques now.

Monkey is the warden of a prison, but not just any ordinary prison. It's a jail solely for time-travel criminals and the inmates include Napoleon. In the pilot episode, Monkey gathers the prisoners together in the exercise yard and orders them to build go-karts from old bits of scrap that are lying around, as the guards (played by the sexy women from *Birds of a Feather*) oversee their efforts. With hilarious consequences, obvs.

There's a lot going on there and I don't want the title to be too vague, so I think we'll just call it 'The Monkey Show'.

See you at the Baftas!

Monkey   **Pretty Actress**

– Chapter Seven –

Romantic Comedy

Ah, the cinema. Also known as the movies. Or the pictures. Or the silver screen. Or the great big rectangle of dreams. Okay, so it's mostly just me who calls it that, but I hope I've made my point.

Is there anything finer than watching a funny film at the cinema? A room full of complete strangers, all united in their glee at what they're seeing on the big screen. Roaring and snorting together, spitting fizzy drinks, nachos and popcorn everywhere, as tears of jocular joy stream down their faces. It's fantastic.

If a team of aliens were to come down to Earth, wander into a cinema and see hundreds of us completely losing it to Ron Burgundy's immortal jazz-flute performance in *Anchorman*, they'd recoil, realising that nothing is more powerful than collective hilarity. They would hastily retreat back to their home planet, knowing that we could never be conquered.

I think what I'm saying here is that if we all keep laughing at hilarious films, we'll never end up as slaves to a hostile invading race from some unknown, faraway planet. There, take that thought and keep it in your special place.

Not *that* special place.

In recent years, there's been one genre of comedy movie that has done more than just grabbed and shaken around our laughter glands – it's stolen our hearts as well. I speak, of course, of the romantic comedy, or the romcom, as the lazy speakers among us have come to call it.

The romcom has almost killed off the 'com' as we know it. These days, if we take our seats in the cinema and watch a com that has

no rom, we're likely to shout, "But where's the rom?" at the screen before marching out of the auditorium and demanding a full refund. "That com has no rom in it," we'd cry, as the cinema manager nods sympathetically before handing back our money.

How did we get here? Here are my favourite ever romcoms. Snuggle up and go all gooey-eyed as we LOL our way through them together.

WHEN HARRY MET SALLY... (1989) Ahhh, possibly *the* classic modern romcom, with 50% rom and 50% com (trust me, I tested it very thoroughly). Can a man and a woman who are just friends ever become romantically entangulated with one another? The film is only a quarter of a century old and you might not have even seen it yet, so I don't want to give away the surprise ending, but [SPOILER ALERT!] Yes, they can. Of course, this is also the film which contains *that* scene in the diner. You know the one – where Sally does her 'wolf howling at the moon' impersonation, bringing the whole place to a silent standstill. All except for one old lady, who says, "I'll have a tuna sandwich!" Brilliant.

PRETTY WOMAN (1990) I was very young when I first saw this one, but it left a lasting impression on me. Basically, Richard Gere's character is a slave trader, who wants to buy Julia Roberts' character, so that she can work for him on his love farm. But Julia is a feisty lady and isn't prepared to be bought so easily. She tells him that he can only have her for one night and it'll cost him one million dollars. There's some arguing, he refuses to pay up and she falls in love with him as a result. Genius. There's also the first known sighting of back-to-back standing on the *Pretty Woman* poster. You know, where the two main characters stand together, but are facing away from each other. It's a style that's been copied thousands of times since, and, these days, you won't get a romcom licence from Hollywood without one.

FOUR WEDDINGS AND A FUNERAL (1994)

Conclusive proof that the British, with their tea, jam sandwiches and traditional stiff upper lip could be just like the Americans and combine the twin disciplines of rom and com into a single movie. Although they did chuck an American into it, just in case it all went horribly wrong. Hugh Grant was the star of this one, and was a huge success for years afterwards. British men even changed their seduction techniques, growing their hair all floppy, bumbling about and umming all over the place, pretending they couldn't get their words out in the hope that an American lady would fall in love with them. There's also the interesting 'Duck Face' sub-plot, where a crazed psycho goes on a murderous rampage while wearing a rubber-duck mask. (Mr/Ms Editor, please check and confirm this as it might have been a dream that I had). [Note from Editor: Sounds about right. Note to self, check Wikipedia before uploading to print.]

THERE'S SOMETHING ABOUT MARY (1998)

Two men pursue one woman in this classic romcom, which has 17% more com than rom, according to my scientific studies. It's also got the classic scene where Mary puts a little bit too much hair gel on and goes out of the house looking a bit silly. I literally rolled around in the aisles when I saw that one. So funny!

HOW TO LOSE A GUY IN 10 DAYS (2003)

Undoubtedly the greatest 'leaning back-to-back on the poster' romcom of the 21st century and also starring Matthew McConaughey, who has leaned against the backs of many leading ladies in over 100 films. Andie and Ben are faced with a challenge – to win in the most romantic game of hide-and-seek ever played. Together they try and lose each other over a ten-day period, but become so enthralled that they end up falling in love! There's also the classic scene where Andie finds Ben in a den that he's made in the woods, after a three-day-long, hide-and-seek marathon, helped by the hand-painted 'Ben's Den' sign that he's stuck outside it. This is what happens. Truth. I could be a synopsis writer. No, *you* haven't actually seen *How to Lose a Guy in 10 Days* and *you* are making up stuff about it!

During my time as a Monkey superstar, I've been offered roles in countless romcoms and the reception staff in Hollywood all know me by my first name because they've seen me turn up for so many meetings. But I still haven't found the right project for my specialist talents and I'm not prepared to compromise and work on something that hasn't got the right rom/com balance.

For example, I recently had a discussion about playing alongside Jennifer Lawrence in a romcom, but she was keen to stay in *Hunger Games* mode and insisted on a scene where she chased me through a forest with a bow and arrow. I fail to see what is funny, or romantic about that. Also, she wanted Brad Pitt to have a leading role in the film, playing her boyfriend – I explained that I didn't think that was particularly romantic either.

Then there was another failed project, with me pencilled in to play alongside Penelope Cruz in another romcom, set in outer space. I came up with the story for this one myself and was convinced it could be a genuine classic, but we had a couple of minor creative differences.

We were supposed to play the world's first married couple on the International Space Station, but Penelope wanted her character to be left behind by accident while I was fired off into outer space on my own. She also wanted George Clooney to play my best friend, who she finds love with once my rocket became stranded behind the moon. Hmmm…

So, it seems that my search for the perfect romcom is like my search for the perfect lady in my life – doomed.

But the trick is to never give up.

Ever.

Did you hear about the magic tractor?

It turned into a field.

Come closer, dear reader, and let me tell you the funniest joke that has ever existed. You'll need to be sitting down while you read this, well away from any hard, or sharp objects, and you'd also better make sure that you're not eating, or drinking, anything before you read any further – you wouldn't want to spray food and drink all over the place when we get to the punchline.

Ready? Here we go...

A hamster walks into a bar and says to the bartender, "Will you give me a free beer if I show you something amazing you've never seen before?" The bartender says, "Sure, but it'd better be good." So the man reaches into his pocket and pulls out a hamster... no, wait it's a MAN who walks into the bar, not a hamster. Sorry.

Okay... the man reaches into his coat pocket and pulls out a hamster. He puts the hamster down on the grass, and the hamster runs... hang on, there's no grass, it's a bar.

The man puts the hamster down on the bar and it pulls out a pack of cards and proceeds to shuffle them. The bartender says... erm...

Sorry, bear with me.

I know this. Oh, I've got it mixed up again – the hamster jumps off the bar, onto the piano and starts playing it beautifully. After he's finished, the hamster does a triple somersault and lands back in the man's pocket. To which the bartender says...

"WHY THE LONG FACE?"

Damn. That's the punchline to a different joke. Look, it's probably on the Internet if you really want to know how it goes.

Sorry.

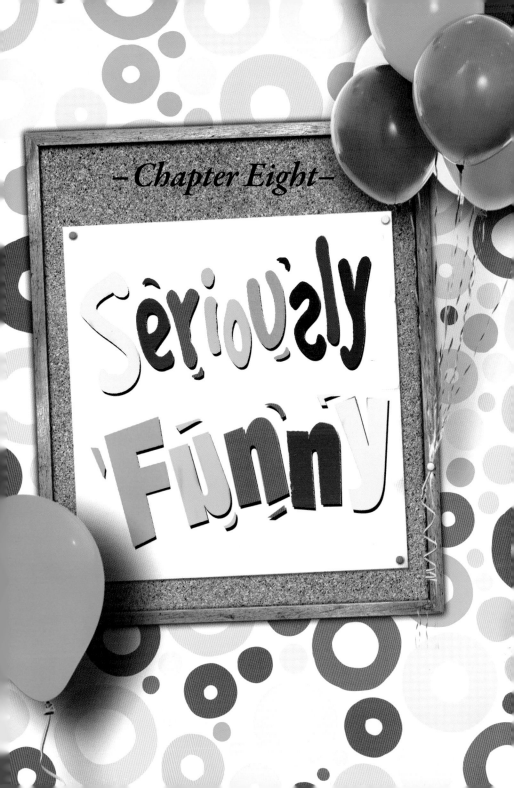

– Chapter Eight –

Seriously 'Funny'

It's a serious world that we live in these days. Read the papers and it's all crime, war, destruction, devastation, depravation and Z-list celebs falling out of cars and being sick. And that's just in my local rag.

The men and women in charge need to lighten up and give us more to smile about. That way we'll be more inclined to vote for them, which is surely what they all want.

When you think about it, politics is just like a slightly bigger version of *Britain's Got Talent*. If you watched the show and were faced with the choice between someone who did loads of impressions and cracked a bunch of jokes, or someone who smashed up the possessions of some poor people in grim silence, who would you vote for?

Exactly.

All is not lost. There are some politicians out there who appreciate that we want to be entertained from time-to-time, while we're being bombarded with tax increases. Here in Britain, we have Boris Johnson, the Mayor of London. A jolly man with a podgy face and fluffy hair, he's never scared to make himself look like a complete oaf, if it'll put smiles on our faces.

Remember the time he went down a zip wire and got stuck in mid-air? Brilliant. Or his many appearances as the guest presenter on *Have I Got News For You?* Hilarious. Or that time when he made a series of comments that offended tens of thousands of Liverpudlians?

Okay, so maybe he doesn't always hit the comedy bullseye.

Americans lead the way in many areas, such as coming up with new flavours for popcorn and inventing lasers, bubblegum and toilet paper, and their politicians are usually funnier than ours as well.

The Bush family has provided us with two generations of presidential LOLs, starting with George Snr., who was responsible for this mumble-mouthed zinger:

"For seven-and-a-half years I've worked alongside President Reagan. We've had triumphs. Made some mistakes. We've had some sex... uh... setbacks."

His good work has been taken to a new level by his son, George W. Bush, a man who it sometimes seemed was struggling with the idea that English was his first language. Among his finest garbled moments are:

"I know the human being and fish can coexist peacefully."

"They misunderestimated me."

"I know how hard it is for you to put food on your family."

"Rarely is the question asked, 'is our children learning?'"

"There's an old saying in Tennessee... I know it's in Texas, probably in Tennessee... that says, fool me once, shame on... shame on you. Fool me... you can't get fooled again."

Perhaps our serious public figures feel they can be funnier if they don't have any real power. One of the reasons the Queen has gandered so much praise and admiration comes from having a lovable rogue by her side. She could have chosen me for that role of course, but she went for dear old Phil. Here are some of the Duke of Edinburgh's greatest hits:

To the President of Nigeria, who was in national dress, "You look like you're ready for bed!"

"A few years ago, everybody was saying we must have more leisure, everyone's working too much. Now everybody's got more leisure time they're complaining they're unemployed. People don't seem to make up their minds what they want."

On Tom Jones, "It's difficult to see how it's possible to become immensely valuable by singing what are the most hideous songs."

To a Scottish driving instructor, "How do you keep the natives off the booze long enough to pass the test?"

To a woman and her guide dog, "Do you know they're now producing eating dogs for the anorexics?"

On London traffic and tourism, "The problem with London is the tourists. They cause the congestion. If we could stop the tourism, we could stop the congestion."

On Princess Anne, 1970, "If it doesn't fart or eat hay, she isn't interested."

123

Maybe the most shockingly funny of all the politicians is Silvio Berlusconi, the former Italian prime minister. He's not allowed to be the PM any more after being convicted for tax fraud, but I wouldn't be surprised if he gave it another try.

The majority of Berlusconi's most notorious quotes are too shocking even for a risqué, grown-up book like this, but this one just about makes the cut:

"When asked if they would like to have sex with me, 30% of women said, 'Yes', while the other 70% replied, 'What, again?'"

Hmmm... you probably wouldn't get that from Gordon Brown.

As I write this, David Cameron is still the prime minister, but you never know when his leadership might be challenged. His prospects of surviving in the job would improve if he would just bring the LOLS a bit more often.

Dave, if you're reading this, or having it read to you at bedtime by one of your minions, I've come up with a few sure-fire ways that could help lighten things up and guarantee you another general election victory.

My lawyers have asked me to add that if you want to use any of the below, you automatically have to make me chancellor after you've won the election. And I get to present the Budget while wearing a dressing gown. On horseback.

1. Work on a catchphrase. Your, "We're all in it together" is pretty good, but it needs more. You should look over your shoulder at your cabinet ministers and say something like, "Am I right, or am I right?" as well, in a funny Yorkshire accent. Try to avoid reviving "Loadsamoney!" though.

2. Get a hand puppet as a sidekick. Maybe one that looks like Ed Miliband. Call him Little Ed and pretend that he's whispering things in your ear during *Prime Minister's Questions*. Everyone will love that.

3. Use George Osborne as your sidekick. Make him wear funnier clothes, maybe a red wig, and make fun of him, like Eric Morecambe did to Ernie Wise.

4. Props. Get a flower in your buttonhole that squirts water across at Ed Miliband (or the new Labour leader, delete as appropriate). Squirt it again, just when he's wiped it off his face. Comedy is all about timing.

5. Get stuck in for Comic Relief. Do one of those amazing physical feats that celebrities like to do to help raise millions. Perhaps you could carry Boris Johnson up the Shard?

– *Chapter Nine* –

ANIMAL KINGDOM OF COMEDY

A nimals. Are they the friends of humans, or the enemies? Perhaps they're somewhere in between – the frenemies, if you like. Mmmm, I'm glad we've sorted that out so early into the chapter, aren't you?

Whether you love them, or hate them (and as a monkey, I know which side I'm firmly on), you can't deny that our furry, scaly friends are always a great source of LOLs and ROFLs.

Well, I say always, but perhaps some creatures are funnier than others? I've compiled a quick, handy guide in order to help you tell between the rib-tickling comedians and the laughter-free losers of the animal kingdom.

CATS Kings of the jungle… the Internet jungle that is. If cats didn't exist, I don't think that the World Wide Web would either. It's estimated that 65% of the Internet is made up of funny, or cute, pictures of cats. Cats that have somehow fitted their entire bodies inside glass jars, cats dressed up as pirates, cats driving tiny cars – all of that stuff. Imagine Michael McIntyre if he was a cat. You can't, because the idea is almost *too* funny. Good work, cats – keep it up.

Funny-o-meter rating: 95%

DOGS Poor dogs. We used to think they were funny when they went on TV and said, "Sausages", but then the cats came along and stole all of their thunder. Also, dogs don't help themselves by repeatedly breaking wind, or licking parts of their bodies that really shouldn't be licked, especially when they do it while your elderly auntie is visiting and nibbling on a Victoria sponge.

Funny-o-meter rating: 69%

HORSES Yep, they're funny in pantomimes, but (SPOILER ALERT) that's just two humans in a suit… so get over it. Are horses funny in real life? No, because they're so potentially dangerous – giant unwieldy beasts that aren't in complete control of their bodies, hence the need for jockeys. Like a tiny dinosaur on roller skates, you can never be truly at ease whenever a horse is in the room.

Funny-o-meter rating: 18%

COWS There's no real history of cows in comedy, although there was that craze a few years ago, when drunk students used to tip them over in fields. Sadly, the things that drunk students find funny are rarely actually funny to anyone else. Sorry, cows.

Funny-o-meter: 9%

ELEPHANTS Hmmm, perhaps animals aren't that comical after all. Yes, there's their funny trunks, and conjuring up the image of two elephants 'getting it on' is always amusing, but that's about it.

Funny-o-meter: 23%

PENGUINS Ah, this is more like it! Penguins walk funny, they slide around on ice funny and they've got wings instead of arms and have to pick things up with their beaks – funny. On the downside, they make unpleasant noises and they stink, but if they work hard on honing their act and start being more cute on the Internet, I can see a bright future for this lot.

Funny-o-meter: 55%

ANTS Don't be ridiculous. Yes, we're impressed by their constant scurrying and the way they carry around crumbs that are bigger than their own bodies, but they'll never really make us laugh.

Funny-o-meter: 4%

PANDAS No, there's nothing to see here either. Just enormous, lazy, bamboo-chewing versions of ants when you think about it.

Funny-o-meter: 4%

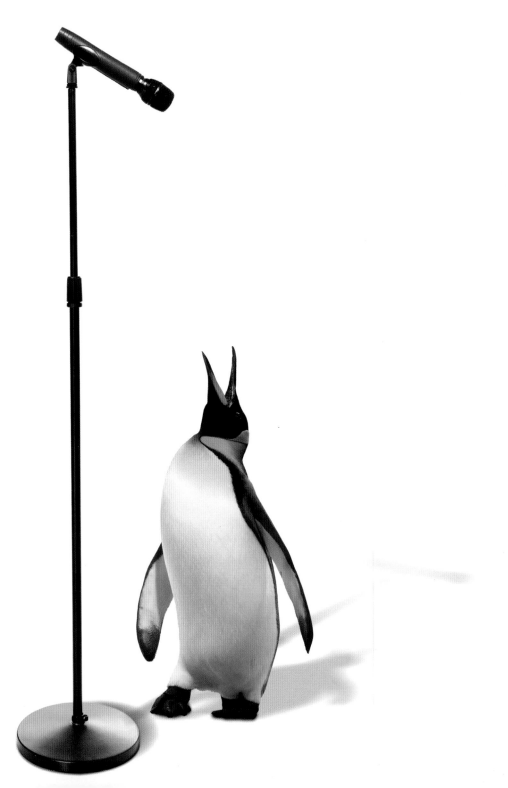

MONKEYS Ah now, *this* is more like it. The monkey is without doubt the funniest animal on the planet. So many different types and each one with a different comedic hallmark. There's the baboon with its red bottom, the orang-utan with its long, swinging arms and spiky-haired babies, the chimpanzee with the tea parties, the howler

monkey with its howling, and all the others with their poo-throwing. You can say that I'm biased if you like, but I might give one of these fellas a call and get him to come round and throw poo at you if you do.

Funny-o-meter: 100%

So, cats and monkeys aside, it looks as though the jury is out on whether animals are funny, or not. We're going to need some more specific evidence if we're going to crack this one. Luckily, I've been down the library with a flask of tea and a few packets of biscuits, and I've put together my AMAZING AMUSING ANIMAL AWARDS!

BEST MUSICAL MOGGIES This award goes to The Musashis, a five-piece group of cats who have become huge in Japan after singing a string of Christmas and New Year songs. They're well-rewarded too, and receive a large skipjack tuna for every song they record.

MIRACLE CAT AWARD This one is for an unnamed, lost cat that managed to find his way to an animal rescue centre in Fife, Scotland… WITH A TIN OF CAT FOOD STUCK ON HIS FACE! No one knows how he made it there, and he even managed to navigate a busy road on the way. Okay, so it's more of an incredible story than a funny one, although the tin of food stuck on his face would have been pretty chuckleworthy.

FRIENDLIEST FOX AWARD The winner of this one is nameless because he's an urban fox, but he's one with a conscience. Back in 2012, the unnamed furry thief stole a woman's handbag in a car park in Burgess Hill, West Sussex, and ran off towards the nearest bush with it. But, he quickly saw the error of his ways and returned it almost immediately, dropping it at the owner's feet and slinking off. Good work, Foxy! It's never too late to turn your back on a life of crime.

PREMIUM PAMPERED POOCH AWARD People say that dogs often look like their owners and miniature pinscher Lu Lu would have fitted into that category – if her owner enjoyed tottering around their home city of Zhumadian in China with a teddy bear bag on his arm. For reasons best known to herself, that is what Lu Lu is into, with no training, or encouragement whatsoever. Takes all sorts.

MOST FOOTLOOSE FELINE Sergeant Podge was a well-travelled cat who used to go out at night and appear exactly one-and-a-half miles away from home every morning. His owner, Liz Bullard, would pick him up from the same spot every morning in her car. Now that I come to think about it, this story is more 'funny peculiar' than 'funny ha-ha'.

WILDEST RODEO MONKEY Ladies and gentlemen, I give you Whiplash the Cowboy Monkey, a 27-year-old capuchin monkey who has been riding on the backs of dogs ever since he was two years of age. I've seen him in action and can confirm that he is without doubt the funniest animal I've ever witnessed. Whiplash's website boasts that he is the 'three-time Pro-Rodeo Entertainer of the Year'. Hang on – only three times? I demand a recount!

There we are then – there's no doubt whatsoever that animals are funny. What's more, I'm now off to ring my publisher and pitch them the idea of a *Monkey's Funniest Animals* book. I can almost smell the glory and the awards already!

Why did the scarecrow win an award?

Because he was outstanding in his field.

fopdoodle

1. (obsolete) A stupid or insignificant
A fool; a simple monkey.
plural: fopdoodles

– *Chapter Ten* –

Here are my all-time favourite, funny, unusual, or plain-weird words, along with some examples of how to use them. Let's bring these brillilicious words back!

Absquatulate – to leave, or abscond with something. As in, "Monkey, I have just absquatulated with your shampoo and conditioner."

Allegator – someone who alleges. As in, "I am an allegator. I am alleging that you are hiding an alligator in the boot of your car. That is my allegation."

Argle-bargle – a loud row, or quarrel. As in, "I'm prepared to put up with argle and I'm reasonably tolerant of bargle, but what I will not stand for is argle-bargle. Okay?"

Batrachomyomachy – making a mountain out of a molehill. As in, "Look, Monkey, highlighting that I put slightly too much vinegar on your chips is simply batrachomyomachy."

Bloviate – to speak pompously, or brag. As in, "Here comes Roger – it won't be long before he bloviates about his new electric toothbrush again."

Borborygmus – a rumbling of the stomach. As in, "I'm suffering from extreme borborygmus right now and I'm going to need a pie."

Bumbershoot – an umbrella. As in, "Looks like it's about to rain. Before I head out to the opera later, I shall select my finest bumbershoot from my extensive collection."

Canoodle – to hug and kiss. As in, "I've got us back-row seats at the opera so that we can canoodle. I'll let you hold my bumbershoot if you're lucky."

Cockalorum – a small, haughty man. As in, "Here comes the mayor. What a horrible, old cockalorum he truly is."

Cockamamie – absurd, outlandish. As in, "Look at him swaggering along, with his chains and silly, cockamamie hat perched on his head. What a horrible, old cockalorum that mayor truly is."

Codswallop – nonsense, balderdash. As in, "Listen to the codswallop that is coming out of his mouth, while he perches that silly, cockamamie hat on his head. What a horrible old, cockalorum that mayor truly is."

Collop – a slice of meat, or fold of flab. As in, "Care for some collop? In a bun?"

Crapulence – discomfort from eating, or drinking, too much. As in, "Ooooooh, I think I've eaten too much collop and now I've got a nasty case of crapulence."

Crudivore – an eater of raw food. As in, "Monkey is a crudivore. He doesn't believe in cooking his collop first."

Donnybrook – a melee, a riot. As in, "There was quite a donnybrook in the bookshop as people fought to get their hands on a copy of Monkey's latest book."

Doozy – something really great. As in, "I'm so glad I prevailed in the bookshop donnybrook. This new Monkey book is a doozy!"

Dudgeon – a bad mood, a huff. As in, "I'm in a bit of a dudgeon as I've accidentally dropped my Monkey book down the toilet."

Fartlek – a type of athletic training regime. As in, "Monkey looks all set to win a record ten gold medals at the Woollen Olympics, all thanks to his strenuous fartlek."

Firkin – a quarter barrel, or small cask. As in, "I'm so thirsty I could drink a firkin of fizzy pop!"

Folderol – Nonsense. As in, "I didn't like that new book by Monkey. It was full of folderol from start to finish." (*Note*: no one has ever said that sentence in the history of the world.)

Fuddy-duddy – an old-fashioned, mild-mannered person. As in, "Monkey is becoming such a fuddy-duddy these days. I wouldn't be surprised if he started wearing an old-fashioned furbelow."

Furbelow – a fringe, or ruffle. As in, "Monkey arrived at the film premiere wearing a furbelow and looking very much like a fuddy-duddy."

Gardyloo – a warning shouted before throwing water from above. As in, "Gardyloo! Whoops, sorry… it means I'm about to throw some water down from above. Can I get you a towel?"

Gastromancy – fortune-telling from the rumblings of the stomach. As in, "My gastromancy skills tell me that you will soon be suffering from an acute dose of crapulence."

Gobbledygook – nonsense, balderdash. As in, "I thought this chapter would just be a load of old gobbledygook, but it's not too bad so far."

Hemidemisemiquaver – a musical timing of $\frac{1}{64}$. As in, "Monkey was surprised when his album of songs, played entirely in hemidemisemiquavers, failed to top the charts."

Hoosegow – a jail, or prison. As in, "You are under arrest for stealing Monkey's furbelow from his washing line. You'll do some hard time in the hoosegow for this!"

Jackanapes – a rapscallion, hooligan. As in, "The furbelow-stealing jackanapes laughed with contempt as he was threatened with some hard time in the hoosegow."

La-di-da – an interjection indicating that something is pretentious. "'Oooh, la-di-da,' said Monkey, as Al crooked out his little finger while sipping his cup of tea."

Lollygag – to move slowly, fall behind. As in, "Monkey lollygagged his way through the marathon. Perhaps dressing up as a *Tyrannosaurus rex* hadn't been the smartest idea he'd ever had."

Mugwump – an independent politician who does not follow any party. "Although he was a mugwump, Monkey expected to be elected as an MP, so that he could work for the cause of woollen characters."

Mumpsimus – an outdated and unreasonable position on an issue. "Monkey's attempt to get Parliament to vote for a free horse and carriage for every woollen character was regarded as mumpsimus."

Nincompoop – a foolish person. As in, "Monkey decided not to stand for a second term as an MP after 97% of his constituents agreed that he was a nincompoop."

Pandiculation – a full-body stretch. As in, "Monkey awoke, yawned, performed a pandiculation and then reached for the tea-maker by his bed."

Pettifogger – a person who tries to befuddle others with his speech. As in, "By using all of the words in this chapter on a daily basis, Monkey is becoming quite the pettifogger."

Quean – a disreputable woman. As in, "I'll tell you who's definitely not a quean – the Queen."

Ranivorous – frog-eating. As in, "The ranivorous teenager threw himself into the lake in an attempt to catch some dinner."

Sialoquent – one who spits while speaking. As in, "Scores of people fled from the sialoquent, ranivorous teenager as he messily boasted about his frog-eating antics."

Smellfungus – a perpetual pessimist. As in, "'Stop being such a smellfungus,' said Monkey, as Al refused to go outside in case the sky fell in."

Snollygoster – a person who can't be trusted. As in, "Monkey suspected that the man who was trying to sell him magic beans at the market might have been a snollygoster."

Tatterdemalion – a person in rags. As in, "Monkey took pity on the tatterdemalion who was sitting by the side of the road, and handed him the magic beans he had just paid £35 for."

Vomitory – an exit, or outlet. As in, "'That's ironic,' thought Monkey, as he stepped over the puddle of sick on the floor of the vomitory."

Knock, Knock! Thanks...

I'd like to thank the following people for helping me make this book as brilliant as my last one!

Andy Dawson, Kristen Whitley, Ian York, Mother and everyone at Comic Relief

Monkey - Nigel Plaskitt, Susan Beattie and Ben Miller
Monkey and costumes created by Paul Jomain